Management by Idiots

This book captures the wisdom-steps taken by the author on his way to becoming the youngest CEO of a Public Sector Enterprise in India and eventually CEO of one of the largest organizations in the world.

Written for today's reader who is hard-pressed for time, the book is organized into short and lucid chapters dotted with enriching thoughts and striking illustrations driving the messages deeper.

A straight-out-of-the-heart presentation of insights acquired during three and a half decades of learning the ropes and growing as a successful business leader, *Management by Idiots* reaches out to anybody willing to think differently: students, young executives, people seeking leadership positions, and anybody striving to cope with the demands of the corporate world.

'This book will be really a good inspiration to ... young technocrats particularly. Practical tips [on] ... how to handle a situation. And the tips to handle situation means mainly the tips to handle the people who are manning the situations. That is what he has been telling.'

Padma Vibhushan Dr E. Sreedharan

'Dr Roy Choudhury's book is an easy and engaging read. It reflects his rich practical experience and varied interests. He has used a range of references, from Hindi films to great philosophers to cricket, to make the book entertaining as well as insightful.'

Padma Bhushan Chanda Kochhar, MD & CEO, ICICI Bank Limited

'To say something which can be comprehended by the common people, it requires tremendous amount of endowment. That's where I find the language fascinating ... it flows in a rhythmic fashion like a river. And I say that it's a great book'

Padma Shri Dr Pritam Singh

'In his book, Arup Roy Choudhury focuses on leading without fear'

The Economic Times

'[This book] is a crisp composition of real life anecdotes spread into 20 chapters ... The author links them [common sayings] up with management lessons'

The Hindu-Business Line

'The book is an account of the author's vast experience in life'

Press Trust of India

Management by Idiots

'Don't let schooling interfere with your education'—Mark Twain

Arup Roy Choudhury

McGraw Hill Education (India) Private Limited
NEW DELHI

McGraw Hill Education Offices

New Delhi New York St Louis San Francisco Auckland Bogotá Caracas
Kuala Lumpur Lisbon London Madrid Mexico City Milan Montreal
San Juan Santiago Singapore Sydney Tokyo Toronto

McGraw Hill Education (India) Private Limited

Published by McGraw Hill Education (India) Private Limited,
P-24, Green Park Extension, New Delhi 110 016

Management by Idiots

Seventh reprint 2015
RDLYCRZVRZXCL

Print Edition:
ISBN-13: 978-93-5134-297-7
ISBN-10: 93-5134-297-2

Ebook Edition
ISBN-13: 978-93-5134-298-4
ISBN-10: 93-5134-298-0

Managing Director: *Kaushik Bellani*
Publishing Manager—Professional: *Mitadru Basu*
Manager—Production: *Sohan Gaur*
DGM—Sales and Business Development—Professional: *S. Girish*
Asst. Product Manager—BGR: *Priyanka Goel*
General Manager—Production: *Rajender P Ghansela*
Manager—Production: *Reji Kumar*

Typeset at Script Makers, 19, A1-B, DDA Market, Paschim Vihar, New Delhi 110 063 and text and cover printed at Sanat Printers, 312, EPIP, HSIDC, Kundli, Sonepat, Haryana

Illustrator: Irfan

Cover Design: Mukul Khattar

Visit us at: www.mheducation.co.in

To

those who are willing

to think out-of-the-box

Contents

Acknowledgements

I deeply acknowledge My Guru Maharaj Jee, Sree Sree Mohananand Brahmachari who instilled in me the spirit of 'Sankalpa Shuddha hi Siddha' and cultivated my value system and convictions which have enabled me to reach where I am today. I dedicate my life and my work at his lotus feet.

My mother who was a catalyst for the paradigm shift on how we siblings toddled and wobbled our way through the stage and age where every act needed someone to dream for us and hold our hand. Most importantly, for finding for us our guiding light, our Guru Maharaj Jee.

My father (late Dhirendranath) and father-in-law (late Saroj Kumar Mitra) who were self-made men from the first generation of post-Independence Indians, achieving soaring heights in their own fields and contributing so much to what I am today.

My mother-in-law who had faith and admiration for whatever I did and spared no pains to demonstrate her affection; my wife Sharmila and son Shyamrup who, I am sure, think that I am a little crazy, but love me and support me from the bottom of their hearts.

All the unsung people who inspired and supported me.

And McGraw Hill Education for bringing the work to light.

Why this book?

Not for a moment and not by a long shot do I consider myself anywhere close to being a management guru. Nor do I qualify to teach management lessons.

Much before I came across this powerful German maxim, '*Nur der Handelndelernt*', 'the doer alone learneth', it had been my guiding principle.

All my 'academic' pursuits are but offshoots of what I do in the gritty world of work.

In school, I was never among those outstanding students who would consider themselves to be the cat's whiskers and strut around with lordly disdain about their less celebrated fellow students. Barring occasional spurts of brilliance, my educational pursuits have been generally mundane, even humdrum at times. But I was always a cheerful learner without any 'chip on my shoulder'.

How do you describe a book written by such a guy? Selecting a name to describe this audacious foray into the territory of printed words was a big problem for me. I am happy that I found a name to describe the gumption that this book is all about, 'Management by Idiots'.

Preserving 'idiocy' is the central idea of Mark Twain's plea, 'Don't let schooling interfere with your education'. Experts on creativity also highlight the need to preserve the 'child' within, to keep lateral thinking flowing, and so on.

The 'over burden' of pre-packaged management concepts floated from the great business schools in the West has to be accumulated. It has its own value and utility. But after learning these concepts, we must also 'un-learn' them. This un-learning enables one to deal with the unique and specific business situations with spontaneity, authenticity and 'guts'. Being 'gutsy' may be same as being an idiot. So be it. It works! It works big time! It has worked for me. It has worked for quite a few successful business leaders I know at a personal level. It may work for you too.

My friends, colleagues and mentors (some of them prominent Indians) encouraged me into believing that I must be doing some right things for me to head one of the largest power companies in the world. That too, with a fair measure of success, in their opinion.

Many policymakers, decision-makers, business leaders, academics and those in the seminar and conference-circuit conspired to have me speak at a large number of events on an equally large number of topics on management over the years.

I thought of putting together a straight-out-of-the-heart, jargon-free, down-to-earth account of the wisdom acquired through passionate hard work along my way to positions of heading large organizations for about fifteen years so far. Time and again, this wisdom has been validated in live situations.

'To be both a speaker of words and doer of deeds' is an ideal I find much easier to pursue than adding 'a writer of books' to the already daunting range of engagements made more difficult by my lack of credentials.

This book is an effort to reach out to those who retain their humility to benefit from the experience of a fellow practitioner in the field of management which, I believe, is more of an art than a science. This is also meant for those who are beginning to learn the ropes.

My journey finds its beginning in my family moving to Patna in the 1920s. This erstwhile capital of the Mauryan Empire has a lot to offer to the making of modern India as well. I look far beyond mere symbolism when I see that we owe our National Emblem, the 'Lion Capital of Ashoka', to the great Mauryan Emperor whose reign marks one of the most enlightened and glorious epochs in Indian history.

My paternal grandfather belonged to the landowning (Zamindar) class of Taki in today's West Bengal and had to leave home under adverse family circumstances due to the sudden death of his father. He did not tell us enough about his immediate ancestors probably to shield us from the trauma which he himself had to endure.

My father graduated from Patna Engineering College in 1950 and was the topper of the public service commission examination that year. He joined the Bihar Government.

My mother came from the Zamindar family of Bagerhat in Khulna, now in Bangladesh. Her forefathers trace their descent from Raja Pratapaditya, the ruler of the territories of undivided Bengal, Bihar and Odisha of that time.

The Partition was a great leveler!

My grandfather and father built up from scratch everything that we have in what we now call our home town—Patna.

I went to arguably one of the best schools of our times in India, St. Xavier's High School, Patna and St. Michael's High School, Patna. Yes, it is one school! We had to laterally and literally shift from St. Xavier's campus next to the Lawn (Gandhi Maidan) to St. Michael's at Digha Ghat in 1968-69 because the political dispensation at that time was not comfortable with an 'English' school located next to the Lawn.

The school has produced eminent political leaders, diplomats, civil servants, police officers, technocrats, and business and corporate leaders who are doing very well in India and abroad, and I bask in their glory.

Since the time I was old enough to register and comprehend what I saw and heard, I have tried to find some learning in all of that.

My first teacher was Guru Maharaj Jee Sree Sree Mohananand Brahmachari. His father was a civil servant, but he chose the spiritual path and joined his spiritual master, Guru Sree Balananda Brahmachari at Deoghar, in today's Jharkhand state of India. In a subtle way he taught me management through his '*Bani*' or words of wisdom.

Imagine the words of spiritual wisdom being relevant to the world of commerce and business!

Is it not the misadventure of an 'idiot' to think so?

'*Sankalpa Shuddha hi Siddha*' (If your intention is pure, you are bound to succeed) is something which He learnt from His Guru and passed on to us. This is the guiding mantra of my journey and, I am sure, of so many of us. It is just that we have never thought of it in that way.

Let me sign off with recollections of a signage one often comes across while driving along the roads winding up the hills and mountains in India. Probably put up by the Border Roads Organization, it reads, 'If you like what you see, tell others. If you do not like it, tell us.' If you like this book tell your friends and colleagues about it. If you do not like it or want me to improve upon something, then please write to me at mbi2013@yahoo.com or mbiarup@gmail.com.

Management by Idiots

WILLPOWER

1

Jo dar gaya samjho mar gaya

He who gets scared is as good as dead

The immense impact of this dialogue from one of the most popular movies from India is because in a very simple, yet dramatic, way it captures a strong truth which goes beyond the specific context of the movie.

'*Jo Dar Gaya Samjho Mar Gaya*' has the ring of a universal truth about it. The film in which this dialogue features was made nearly four decades ago, in the mid-1970s. But even today, this evergreen dialogue is variously quoted in commercial advertisements and informal conversations. It appears as if its charm will continue to hold sway over future generations also. It essentially says that if there is fear of death, fear of failure, fear of taking risk, fear of coming out of your house, fear of getting exposed to the external environment, you can never enjoy success. A person full of fear is avoided by one and all. So, the idea is to conquer fear and become fearless.

The spirit of fearlessness finds immortal expression in the words of Nobel Laureate Rabindranath Tagore:

Ami bhoy korbona bhoy korbona
Du bela marar aage morbona bhai morbona
Torikhana baite gele majhe majhe tuphan mele
Tai bole hal chere diye dhorbona, kannakati korbo na

I shall not fear,
Never shall I fear.
I shall die but only once,
Not everyday.
While rowing the boat,
One does face storms at times,
But I shall not let go of the oars,
I shall not cry in despair!

William Shakespeare also said:

> 'Cowards die many times before their deaths,
> the valiant never tastes of death but once.'

Our scriptures teach us that if an individual has overcome the fear of death, she can face any challenge. Here, 'death' does not mean physical death. This 'death' occurs in various forms in a person's life.

Fear of failure, of fall from grace and other extreme anxieties create death-like situations. These situations are morbid and grim. Such a debilitating fear kills the appetite for risk. And without risk there can hardly be any gain.

Therefore, one has to come out of such anxieties that constrain our decision-making and risk-taking ability. Then the decision you have taken and the path you have chosen would be correct and smooth.

Professional life is all about travelling on a road which leads you to a series of Y-forks. It is important that a person undertakes a thorough analysis before he decides to adopt one of the two choices at the Y-forks of his professional journey.

The perspective of this 'Y-fork analysis' can be derived from your own experiences—experiences of people whom you have seen and observed in life, or even from the failures you have encountered. Thus, the factors you relied on for decision-making would guide you to a way forward. It should not, at any stage, be an impulsive decision. Nor should it be taken on the basis of blind faith.

Once a decision has been taken, one has to hold firm, even if initial results are contrary to expectations.

When fearless conviction propels your decision, you are on the right path. Abraham Lincoln captures this truth in his inimitable words, 'Be sure you put your feet in the right place, then stand firm.'

In one of the greatest songs ever written, Tagore says:

Jodi tor daak shune keu na ashe
Tobe ekla cholo re

If they answer not to thy call, walk alone.

This is an inspiring song and also a sound management advice.

Pioneers walk alone.

The brave go it alone.

The whole world may not be willing to follow you. But, if there is strength in your conviction, you will find your own path.

This dictum does not mean that you take impulsive or irrational decisions or create situations that are clearly insurmountable.

The whole world is not expected to support you in your endeavours. But, in case you move forward and do not succeed, introspection is absolutely necessary so that the mistake is not repeated in future.

Those who do not learn from history are doomed to repeat it.

Remember, the early bird always catches the worm. But it is the second bird which has the experience of the first bird before it to help select the correct path. It does not mean that you will be a late bird.

You will never be able to take a business enterprise to higher levels unless you have an entrepreneurial streak within you.

It is important that one becomes fearless while taking decisions.

But between fearlessness and misadventure, there is a very thin line which must never be crossed.

At certain stages in life, be it as the head of a family or of a business, you have to take decisions.

As you progress, you will encounter many hurdles that will affect your momentum. This has to be tackled with the help of business acumen, learning, teachings and intuition.

There will also be obstacles put up by those who do not want you to succeed.

These jealousy induced irritants remain at the back of the mind, and thinking continuously about it takes one two steps backward to the one step taken forward.

Once you have risen above the fear of being wronged by others, you go forward fearlessly. You do not allow negative vibes from those who are jealous of you to take root within your system and affect your faith and conviction.

It is mind over matter.

Mind is the ruler of body and aids the soul. Mind is the creator of your destiny. Therefore, it is important that you take control of your mind, and make it fearless. Then you would be able to control physiological and other consequences of fear.

Many people are surprised to look back and find that they had been able to achieve things which they themselves had thought impossible.

The mind-stuff called willpower or determination shapes your destiny. It is not the other way around.

It is said that a famous palmist, after closely looking at Napoleon's palm, told him that he had no fate line which meant he would not achieve anything great. Napoleon drew his sword, lacerated his palm and created a fate line. It is said that after he became the greatest conqueror, he showed his palm to the same palmist and asked how his fate line looked.

The value of such stories contained in our collective memory lies in their inspirational value and not in their historical accuracy.

Your mind creates your destiny which gets reflected in your fate line. I would like you to really keep looking at your palm, from time to time. All it takes is a rudimentary knowledge of palmistry. You will find that your lines have been changing and evolving from time to time as you grow in life. You will find that your mind which has been instrumental in guiding your entire existence towards a certain direction finds reflection in your development on personal and professional fronts. All this gets reflected in the respective lines in your palm. You need not follow Napoleon and create a gash in your palm! Make your mind strong and make your body follow your mind.

In the Indian system of thought we refer to '*Samskara*'. The word 'Samskara' can be described as education, cultivation and training of the mind. It can also mean impressions on the memory and influences on the conduct of a person. 'Samskara' also denotes purification by refinement or education. Drawing upon these meanings, the philosophical traditions of India used the word 'Samskara' to describe impressions embedded on the subconscious mind by past experiences and desires. In the context of western thought, they refer to 'Conscience'. 'Samskara' is something that we derive from our parents and grandparents, relatives and gurus as we grow up. 'Samskara' is also something that we observe and acquire from our environment and surroundings.

A strong mind grounded in good 'Samskara' would reject negativity and filter the environmental inputs in such a fashion that a positive and clean outlook gets embedded in one's system and mind as strong conscience.

At every stage in your professional and personal life, your conscience provides you a reflection of right and wrong. A clear conscience provides you courage.

A mind immersed in work transcends discomforts and irritants. For example, you are sitting in a room and the electricity supply suddenly gets cut off. The weather being hot, you have switched on the air-conditioner and as the power goes off, suddenly you feel terribly hot and your mind tells you that the power will not be restored before an hour or so. Your body adjusts to the heat after a few minutes and you forget the discomfort and carry on with your activities.

Such feats are achieved with the power of the mind. *Srimad Bhagvad Gita* captures the same truth when it says that you should accept heat and cold, joy and sorrow with equanimity and detachment: शीतोष्ण सुखदुःखेषु समः (*Sheetoshna Sukhdukheshu Samah*).

Similarly, in a business situation, your fearless mind plays an important role in every day decision-making by way of overcoming threats, challenges and obstacles.

WILL DO IT TOMORROW.
IN

2

Kaal kare so aaj kar, aaj kare so ab

Do tomorrow's work today, today's work, now

Kaal kare so aaj kar, aaj kare so ab is a very old saying, also captured in poetry by great poets. The saying remains extremely relevant for any practising manager.

There are a number of wisdom statements with similar messages:

- Procrastination is opportunity's assassin
- Promptness or dispatch is the soul of business
- A stitch in time saves nine
- Never put off till tomorrow what you can do today
- The keen spirit seizes the prompt occasion

Leave alone the world of business where promptness is obviously regarded as a necessity, even in the world of art and literature, many greats underline the virtue of promptness.

To quote Pablo Picasso (from Kim Koning, *Writing Epiphanies in the Brushstrokes of Picasso*):

> 'Only put off until tomorrow what you are willing to die having left undone.'

So, even artists are in favour of 'now or never'.

The higher you go in the management hierarchy the more often you find yourself in situations where uncertainties and problems get thrown at you incessantly.

Any decision or issue which has been left unresolved has two possible repercussions. One, it could snowball into a bigger problem because of the inability of the manager to nip it in the bud. Or, just as the food kept aside gets spoilt and starts smelling, any issue kept pending may create an impression of your being indecisive or inactive, tarnishing your credibility and reputation.

Any civil engineer will tell you that a crack in the embankment of a river, if not plugged and repaired in time, will widen and let the flood waters in to cause disaster. Delay aggravates a harmless trickle into a devastating flood. Promptness proves to be a saviour.

What you need to do on a day must be done on that very day.

It is important for a manager to spend a little time in the morning on his desk to segregate issues into two parts: 'Must be done today' and 'Could be done'.

What must be done for the day has to be disposed off on that very day. If due to some exigencies it could not be done that same day, and it is something which can be handled with the help of modern communication techniques and tools like e-mail, fax, SMS, etc., it should be done during the course of the day before you retire to bed. Otherwise, it is always recommended that in the morning, depending upon every individual's biological and psychological rhythm, one must list out things which cannot be left for later.

While out for morning walk, you may make a mental note of urgent things you must do during the day. Then, you must jot down these 'urgent points' in the noting facility in your communication device (mobile phone, tablet, etc.) or on 'post-it' slips and stick the notes on your table to ensure that these are dealt with first in the morning.

Even if you need to skip some issues which you are not able to sort out, it is recommended that you segregate the most important ones, lest you forget the very important issues which may later snowball into a larger problem for the organization. It always gets harder, if delayed.

Procrastination is a recipe for disaster. Promptness is the tonic and preventive which preempts many a crisis.

'Between fearlessness and misadventure, there is a very thin line which must never be crossed.'

'When fearless conviction propels your decision, you are on the right path.'

Appreciation
Acknowledgement

3

If you can give your people one gift, let it be enthusiasm

Have you ever realized that all your employees are constantly looking up to you for appreciation and acknowledgement of their work?

Have you ever realized that after you had relished a nicely spread lunch at home, your wife expects you to appreciate her culinary skills? How do you express your appreciation? It can be a straightforward praise. It can also be a question about the source of some ingredient used or some question in which approval is inherent.

I am sure, you know very well that when you reach home at the end of a hectic day, your child will be waiting for that small chocolate or a little gift that you might have brought for her.

Similarly, those who manage others at the workplace should actually learn to give small gifts to people who work for them.

These gifts need not always be a physical object. It could be a word of appreciation, a pat on the back, a small 'thank you' note, a small note appreciating a job well done. You can also ask simple questions as to how they accomplished the task.

You will find that by giving positive strokes at the right moment, what you essentially do is generate enthusiasm in the person at work or your child or your wife. And they, in turn, try to please you even more in the future.

Enthusiasm is contagious. An interesting fact about enthusiasm is that the enthused person does not actually expect any appreciation. But appreciation inspires him to further accomplishment. This becomes a virtuous cycle. Your appreciation sets off a series of positive outcomes.

You can see the spring in the gait of your subordinates after you have energized them with positive strokes. You spur them on to higher levels of energy.

Appreciation, leading to enthusiasm, is acknowledged by many experts to be a better motivator than money. They also say that enthusiasm for something makes life worth living. Enthusiasm for work, thus, makes work-life truly meaningful.

It is rightly said that nothing great has ever been achieved without enthusiasm. Also, enthusiasm spells the difference between mediocrity and excellence.

All you want as a manager is that your team performs enthusiastically. Then the team delivers more than what is expected of it, setting higher standards of performance. All your team wants, in return, are the small gifts of appreciation that you normally give them.

It is crucial for managers to realize how important it is to inspire their team by giving such small surprise gifts and keep the whole team charged up and motivated. This inspires them to deliver as per the requirement of the situation and the organization.

Therefore, when you go to your workplace, please try to sense as to what 'gift' each subordinate expects from you. What inspires them into performing even better? What charges them up and motivates them as a team? The wisdom of a manager is in gauging this small, yet extremely important, requirement of each individual in his group. Then they weld together into a cohesive and motivated team. In other words, they become a winning combination.

'Delay aggravates a harmless trickle
into a devastating flood.'

'Procrastination is opportunity's assassin.'

'Enthusiasm spells the difference
between mediocrity and excellence.'

HONK!!
HONK!!
HONK!!
NO HORN PLEASE

4

Horn please!

One of the things that hits an Indian travelling to London or New York for the first time is the silence of bumper-to-bumper traffic stretching for miles. Back home, if our ancient sages were to visit us through some time machine, they would be bewildered at the din and bustle of the noisy traffic around what were once their ashrams.

We, the people of India, have become the residents of a 'Horn Please' country. Anyone travelling on our roads is all too familiar with the 'Horn Please' graffiti at the back of many trucks.

We have grown up with this 'Horn Please' mindset. Ironically, we have become a very loud people crowding about in the wonderland of 'Nirvana' that is India. In our land of 'pushers make movers', even a mother, as the saying goes, will not feed her baby unless the infant lets out a loud cry. This phenomenon continues through our adolescence and adulthood to our professional lives. Therefore, we must learn to blow the horn to remove the obstacles we find on the road to achieving our goals.

The psychology of an Indian manager and the features of his work environment cannot be compared with the behavioral norms and organizational climate in the western world.

Irrespective of your level in the hierarchy, you have to proactively make demands to get things done and to make things happen.

The truck driver knows his destination and weaves his way through the maze of traffic, honking, changing gears, finding the best way to take, blending speed and safety.

The Indian manager should also proactively let the superiors, peers and subordinates know of his intentions, his strategies and his destination as well as the timeline. For this, the manager may have to resort to cajoling, reprimanding, reminding, cautioning and so on.

And yes, honking needs to be done even with superiors in order to move towards the goal. Sometimes, superiors can also be obstacles, often unwittingly, and sometimes, knowingly. Therefore, the need to tactfully align them or push them, depending upon the nuances of the situation!

However, the immense value of being cautious and discreet cannot be over-emphasized when you are applying 'Horn Please' with your superiors.

The truck drivers of India pretty much represent the essential Indian approach of struggling one's hard and long way to the destination through the hostile roads and pot-holed highways amid not too accommodating fellow drivers. No American or European trucker can survive our roads. Similarly, no American or European theory of management can address our very Indian issues in our very unique cultural and organizational milieu.

In your journey to the top, you will find that there are people who need an initial push at every stage in life to make them move. In Hindi, it is called a '*Dhakka*' (push). In management parlance, the acronym KITA (Kick In The Ass!) is used to describe this phenomenon. But, at the same time, there are people who do not need any push in order to perform. You need to understand and segregate them. Different approaches are to be applied to different categories of people. Different strokes for different folks!

Some people become complacent. They are like broken-down vehicles that create slow-downs or jams.

Complacency is a disease and it needs specialized diagnostics and treatment. The levels of complacency at different rungs in the organization are to be assessed. One has to use common sense to choose the tools to drive out complacency. And, if need be, inculcate the fear of God among those for whom only extreme measures work.

To ignite the fire in their belly and make people perform at a never-before pace requires attitudinal and psychological transformation of a fundamental kind. You need to sensitize them about the urgency of the corporate mission in which they are engaged. 'Arousing of corporate zeal' should not be misperceived as 'crying wolves' by such employees. If it gets misperceived, the result will be as bad as that in the story in Aesop's fables. In such a situation, the boss also runs the risk of getting branded as 'Hitler', 'Arrogant', 'Rascal' and 'Idiot' (HARI), as in a popular advertisement.

At the end of the day, your effectiveness in using 'Horn Please' strategy will be understood and acknowledged by your team, peers, superiors and subordinates in the right perspective. You will be seen as a fair and well-meaning professional whose ultimate objective is to get things done in the interest of the organization. People will give way and let you move forward to your ultimate destination.

PROMISE
DELIVER

5

Well done is better than well said

One of the most gifted batsmen in the game of cricket, known for his sense of timing and stroke play, Yuvraj Singh, says:

Jab tak balla chal raha hai, tab tak thaat hai beta.
Jab balla nahin chalega to phir ...
All is hunky-dory as long as runs flow.
When runs cease to flow, then ...

It means that all the luxury, glamour and glory are based only on the runs he churns out. Once the runs stop, everything else will stop.

For a batsman, performance is measured in terms of the runs he scores. This statement by Yuvraj Singh in an advertisement campaign has a very important management lesson underneath.

Action and results are all that matters. In the absence of results, everything else becomes meaningless verbiage.

Every manager must realize that saying too much, opening up too much about his plans and generating high hopes among customers are detrimental to his growth as a management professional because, immediately, aspirations of the receiver are set at a certain standard and anything achieved below that acts as a great disadvantage.

Unless you achieve much more than what you speak, it does not earn you much credit.

It is always better to assess your own capabilities, the capabilities of your team, and be sure to deliver before talking or showing your cards in a group or management meeting.

It is always better to be conservative while speaking in such meetings. Your approach should be such that you are always seen as an over-achiever.

It is, of course, not so easy because people who are senior to you will easily see through it if you set targets which are much lower than what you have achieved earlier.

So it is important for you to look at targets undertaken and achieved by you in the past. Analyze quarterly or yearly targets taken up in the past. Analyze the reasons behind the best results achieved for any quarter or year. Discuss it with your core team which achieved the result and then go well prepared for the meeting.

With this approach, not only will you commit what is achievable but your team will also be with you in making efforts to achieve it. You will state only that which can confidently be done and for which you would already have the commitment of your core team. Thus, there will hardly be any chance of your failure. Rather, you may deliver a little more than the committed target, thus making your position stronger in the organization. You will be appreciated and projected as an over-achiever!

It is better to under-promise and over-deliver. It is obviously bad to over-promise and under-deliver.

Few things are as irksome for the top management as an unfulfilled promise by a manager. So delivering results as promised is a must. Exceeding expectations and promises is even better.

A corollary of this is that your equity as a professional depends on your delivering results consistently.

Sachin Tendulkar, arguably the best and most successful batsman of all time, is reported to have said, 'You are as good as your last innings.'

Even an individual of Sachin's unquestionable supremacy in his area of expertise, is alert against resting on his laurels and highlights the need for making a big score in every outing.

Just as runs must consistently flow from the willow of the batsman, results must be delivered consistently by the business leader or manager. All else is vacuous in the absence of concrete results.

Coming from Benjamin Franklin, the statement 'Well done is better than well said' becomes truly authentic as he made pioneering contributions in a mind-boggling range of areas. Electricity, wave theory of light, meteorology, air cooling, oceanography, music and much more! He invented the lightning conductor, bifocals, the Franklin stove, carriage odometer, and the glass harmonica, among other things. What leaves you completely stumped is that he made this colossal contribution while being one of the founding fathers of the United States of America.

Ben really must have been one hell of a busy man doing it all rather than making advance pronouncements about his ground-breaking accomplishments. Such 'action people' are the right role models for any business leader.

COSTING
PLANNING

6

Jugaad

Creating value out of the valueless

Travelling through rural India, you are very likely to chance upon an ingenious contraption of a transportation device—a flat plank of plywood moving on the road—making you wonder how it moves. It might even appear to have come straight off the pages of mythical stories alongside flying carpets. It is a 'vehicle' called '*Jugaad*'. If you look at this device carefully, you find the handle of a discarded two-wheeler affixed to the front of the plywood and under it, a set of four tyres salvaged from the *kabaadi* (junk dealer) or cannibalized from motor vehicles confiscated and kept in police stations or abandoned by owners. The engine for driving this Jugaad is an ordinary agricultural pump-set an average farmer owns. It mostly runs on kerosene or diesel. It is a very handy and useful form of transport serving villagers really well.

This is the level of ingenuity and entrepreneurship that an ordinary rustic mind in India has.

To harness such ingenuity and to channelize it in day-to-day operations in an organization for project execution or troubleshooting is what is done by managers of Jugaad.

Being open and favourable to Jugaad, you will be able to encourage the spirit of improvisation. This results in less expensive yet very effective solutions.

Jugaad is all about out-of-the-box thinking and using already available resources.

In a hands-on job whenever you find yourself amidst problems which have to be solved to prevent them from becoming critical, it is a good idea to discuss the problems with your team members, even if they are not so well-educated and do not have the kind of sophisticated background that you have. While discussing, you will be surprised to find somebody suggest a Jugaad, somebody else improve upon the

Jugaad and, thus, giving you a fully packaged solution to deal with the tricky situation. More often than not, this would be an original idea and prove very efficient when put to work.

Therefore, do not discount the creativity and utility of an individual who works for you because of his humble background, education, looks and clothes. Unknown to you, he might have a powerhouse of a brain which can solve tricky problems and earn you a pat on the back from the management.

1951-2021
OBITUARY

7

Write your own obituary

People aspire for some kind of completeness in life before death. Completeness, in terms of their own ambitions and ideals.

In fact, people seek immortality, whether they are aware of it or not. Even if we leave aside Woody Allen's audacious wish of gaining immortality in his physical body, people do want to 'live' in the memories of others.

Now split the epic of your life ahead of you into small chapters. Run a mental video of your life in a flash-forward mode. Script the future chapters the way you want them to unfold. More so, the chapters about your life at work because that is where you spend most of your waking hours, your active life.

That is where you are going to be talked about the most.

Then, reword the script in the past tense to make it read as an obituary. Imagine you are given a chance to come back to earth from the dead and listen to people talking about you. What would you like to hear?

If you reflect on your journey of life, you will find you have suffered several 'deaths'.

During the career development of a manager, there are frequent changes in responsibilities, positions, locations, ranks, organizations and so forth.

Every time you get a new assignment, you find yourself in a new environment. You are given a new group of people and a new set of resources.

Your job is to blend the people and resources in such a fashion that you not only complete the task and achieve the targets given to you but also move towards your own individual goal.

It is, therefore, important that when you take any step forward at different stages in your life, you are able to clearly think through the perspective about how you would like to be remembered once you finish the assignment.

This will give you an opportunity to reflect on yourself, your strength and your vision in the context of the assignment given to you and the resources put at your disposal.

You can look at the picture that emerges after such reflection as your alter ego. You can then proceed in such a manner that you command respect and come out with flying colours at the end of the assignment.

For reaching this kind of a state of introspection, you have to be open to change. Human beings need to keep changing for the better with the times.

If you close your eyes for a moment and reflect on the changes that have happened to you at the personal level—from a young undergraduate to where you are today—you would be surprised to find yourself to be a different person from who you were at earlier stages in life. This change could not have happened unless you had the strength to accept criticism, to accept failures, to accept others' perspectives and points of view and to accept the situation that you were in.

Therefore, it also makes sense that every time you get a new assignment, you select a group of subordinates who will work with you during that assignment. Encourage them to give honest feedback about you.

If you remain in the same organization for a long time, people may hesitate to give you truthful feedback. You can assure them by conveying that you would be open to anonymous feedback. These proactive steps may enable you to get feedback, which may be quite revealing! Such feedback will help make major changes in your style of management and that will take you further up in the hierarchy.

The crux of the whole issue is that you must keep yourself open. You must keep yourself grounded. You must believe in your abilities and look for inputs and feedback to strengthen your abilities. You should keep all the doors and windows open in your system to receive ideas, to weed out weaknesses and to fine tune your internal system for continuous betterment.

Most people want to be remembered fondly and respectfully as a benefactor, a good leader, a good human being, a good husband, wife, father, mother and much more.

In the Indian context, while performing your tasks as a manager in the organizational hierarchy, you also assume different roles and arouse special expectations. You are also seen as a father figure, a protective friend and elder by the people you work with. Their lives depend on your approach towards the assignments and the team.

Therefore, a managerial obituary of this kind is no different from a personal obituary written about an individual after his death by others. When you take the useful step of writing your own obituary, you come to know very clearly within yourself as to how you want to be remembered by your colleagues, subordinates, superiors and people who have worked hard for your success.

I CLIMB BETTER WHEN I BEND DOWN.
OH! I CATCH MY BREATH UNDER THAT TREE.

8

Humility is the path to success

Please remember that it is necessary to be humble to succeed in life. It is important to seek the blessings of successful people and learn from them the art of doing well in life.

Isaac Newton, one of the greatest geniuses the world has seen, said, 'If I am anything, which I highly doubt I am, I have made myself so by hard work.'

While you rise higher in your career, visualize your rise as a situation where you are climbing up a steep hill. Create a scenario in your mind that while climbing up the steep hill, you get tired and look for a tree in order to rest for a while under its shade. The tree graciously shelters you under its comforting and cool shade and provides the respite that you need to recharge and get on with the next phase of trekking up the hill.

Now observe two important phenomena. When you go up the hill, you bend down and forward to maintain your body's centre of gravity. Then you come under the tree which stands tall, upright and erect. Can you see any management analogies in these imageries?

Remember, you cannot maintain your equilibrium unless you remain humble while climbing up the career graph. During your career path, do you come across people who shelter you like a banyan tree? Acknowledge their selfless support to you with humility. And when you find other people travelling the same path as you had at earlier phases, see whether you can become that banyan tree for them at various stages of their career growth. This approach will not only help you grow in the organization but will also provide you with the basis of team building and motivation.

Almost every day I come across somebody or the other who thinks that he is the best among his peers. He thinks that he could have achieved what nobody else around him has ever achieved. And, probably, he also thinks that he could have done much better than others. Such feeling is generally caused by a weird yet common blend of arrogance and lack of performance. This kind of feeling always generates negative vibes among such people leading them away from the path of self-actualization.

We Indians are usually very curious and overly concerned about what others, especially successful peers, do. We often try to belittle their success by attributing uncharitable traits to them and leveling vacuous allegations against them.

Every manager working in the corporate environment should pause for a while and reflect not on what he thinks he can achieve but on what others think he can achieve. Your appraisal is never done by you. It is always done by somebody else—your superior, subordinate, peer or a group of people.

However high you may think of or rate yourself, it really does not matter. Therefore, every individual should make an effort to see his worth through the eyes of others, using them as his mirrors.

Even at home, it is not important as to how good a parent or husband or wife you think you are. It is important to know how your children and your spouse think about you.

Assessment begins at home. Start taking honest feedback about yourself from your children, your spouse and other dear ones. This will give you the strength to invite feedback in the world of work from your superiors, peers, subordinates and even from your adversaries.

By taking proactive steps to invite feedback you will be surprised to notice how very much more you have come to know about yourself compared to what you knew of yourself earlier. This may enable you to change your self-portrait with gainful consequences.

Thus, keeping yourself open to feedback from others keeps you grounded. It enables you to have a broader perspective. It helps you get better self-understanding and self-awareness. All these together prevent you from becoming arrogant and help you remain humble.

Great management gurus find humility to be perfectly compatible with fierce resolve and strong leadership. Many leadership theorists have taken fancy to what is called a level-5 leader, who is humble and self-effacing, yet very strong and result-oriented.

'Irrespective of your level in the hierarchy,
you have to proactively make demands to get things done
and to make things happen.'

'To ignite the fire in their belly and make people perform at
a never-before pace requires attitudinal and psychological
transformation of a fundamental kind.'

IN
OUT

9

If you fall in love with your work, you will never have to work for the rest of your life

This expression is based on a very old Chinese saying. Many management gurus have also spoken along similar lines.

The ultimate goal of any individual's life is to find happiness. The ultimate spiritual goal for an individual brought up in the Indian culture is to find *Moksha* (Enlightenment).

Is it possible to create a situation of happiness and enlightenment as a way of life while at work?

Imagine that out of sympathy you picked up a little puppy from a pavement on a chilly winter night and took it home. You created a comfortable little habitat for it. Slowly you got involved in the day-to-day life of the puppy. You taught it manners, you taught it do's and don'ts, you taught it hygiene, you organized the way it lived and you came to love every moment of your interaction with it. You looked forward to the loving playfulness of the puppy early in the morning when you got off your bed and also late in the night when the puppy came and sat by your bedside. You felt happy! You watched the puppy grow into a full-fledged dog. You were involved in every moment of the puppy's growth and its achievements.

Now draw a parallel between this situation and your job. Based on your qualifications and achievements, you were selected for a job. How do you relate to your job? Nurturing it, culturing it, looking forward to its challenges, and enjoying the successes, you eventually reach a situation where you have actually fallen in love with your job like you had fallen in love with your pet.

For a practising manager, it is not at all a very difficult parallel. You have to 'personify' your job into a living and throbbing thing pulsating with possibilities, excitements, challenges and accomplishments. In the example of the puppy growing up you were able to discipline and train it. You have to structure and 'enliven' your job in a way that it meets with the goals of the organization that you have joined. Like in the case of the puppy, when you were totally involved in its growth as also taking care of it during the periods of bad health, you should get totally engaged with your job in a situation of crisis.

You look forward to a situation when everyday in the morning you are charged up for coming to your workplace like a young lover looks forward to meeting his beloved. Similarly, at the end of the day return home from your place of work with a sense of accomplishment, comfort and contentment, setting the stage for the next enjoyable day for which you eagerly wait. If such a 'tug' can be created about your workplace, you are actually in love with your job. When you come to work in the morning, you are so charged up! And at the end of the day when you go home you do not feel tired at all, however much work you did during the day.

It energizes you.

It renews you.

It never tires you.

No thought about love for work can be considered complete without remembering the immortal words of Kahlil Gibran (from *The Prophet*):

And all knowledge is vain save when there is work.
And all work is empty save when there is love. And when you work with love you bind yourself to yourself, and to one another, and to God ...
And what is it to work with love?
It is to weave the cloth with threads drawn from your heart, even as if your beloved were to wear that cloth.
It is to build a house with affection, even as if your beloved were to dwell in that house.
It is to sow seeds with tenderness and reap the harvest with joy, even as if your beloved were to eat the fruit.

Kahlil Gibran wrote these lines extolling the virtue of working with a heart full of love in the era of agrarian societies.

Change the reference points to the post-industrial knowledge economy of today and rewrite the lines for yourself, through your 'labour of love'.

Enjoy the perennial source of energy that your work, nay, your love, is!

'"Action people" are the right role models
for any business leader.'

'It is better to under-promise and over-deliver.'

'Jugaad is all about out-of-the-box thinking and
using already available resources.'

Results
BACK-
GROUND

10

Honour and shame from
no condition rise;
act well your part,
there all the honour lies

—Alexander Pope

In today's management scenario in India we have an increasingly large number of educated, intelligent, eager and energetic boys and girls joining the corporate world from all parts of the country. The human resource manager is no more dependent on individuals from the metropolitan cities only, who belong to a particular social and educational background.

We must realize that unless all segments of Indian society are carried together and work together to actualize the Indian dream, no managerial process or tool can help the business enterprise and, in turn, the country to move to a higher trajectory of growth and development.

Today, as a manager of a company, it is important for you to treat an individual as an individual. You need to value the employee on the basis of his or her commitment to the job, education, capabilities and achievements for the company.

It is important to move out of the clutches of sectarianism, casteism or any kind of 'ism' that bedevils many aspects of the Indian society and politics.

Therefore, when you start as the head of a business enterprise or a department or a profit-centre, you have to remember that each individual who is working in your team has to be judged only by his or her 'act' and not on the basis of his or her background such as the State, the region, the caste or sub-caste he or she belongs to.

Treat them as equals and be seen as a person who treats everyone equally.

Always let your team members know that you follow the spirit of the motto, 'What E'er Thou Art, Act Well Thy Part'.

Let nothing become a barrier to your team members trying to attain glory through right action. Be an alert witness to the exceptional actions and deeds of your employees and never fail to acclaim them.

SIR. It is done.
GOOD JOB.
SIR. I'LL SHOW YOU A PERFECT PLAN TOMORROW.
CEO

11

A good plan today is better than a perfect plan tomorrow

'The perfect is the enemy of the good' is a very useful aphorism, a very helpful maxim. It means that insisting on perfection often results in no benefit at all. The statement is commonly attributed to Voltaire whose famous lines are:

> 'In his writings, a wise Italian
> Says that the best is the enemy of the good.'

Robert Watson-Watt, who developed the early warning radar in Britain to counter the rapid growth of the German air force 'Luftwaffe', propounded a 'cult of the imperfect', for which he stated 'Give them the third best to go on with; the second best comes too late; the best never comes.'

The idea behind the strategy of not waiting for the best is to not take too long, else the battle is lost.

As the saying goes, 'A bird in the hand is worth two in the bush.'

The clock keeps on ticking all the time and the hand that has moved in the clockwise direction cannot be moved back anti-clockwise.

It is in the nature of many ambitious people to aspire for perfection in whatever they do.

Walking down memory lane to your school and college days, you would recall all those occasions when you wanted to give a perfect answer to a question in the examination, but you knew that you had not given a perfect answer.

What would have happened had you not submitted the answer sheet unless you wrote a perfect answer? Ask yourself this question.

You submitted the answer sheet because that was the best answer possible for you to give within the range of your knowledge at that time and within the timeframe given to you for answering that question.

You submitted your answer sheet with that 'best possible' answer. Having submitted that imperfect answer, which did not satisfy you, you had scored more than the pass marks and moved on to the next grade. Had you not given that answer, probably you would have gotten a zero and failed in the examination.

In hindsight, on several occasions you would have come to realise that you had given a lousy answer, after discussing the topic with friends or teachers. Sometimes you find your answers childish in the wake of a greater wealth of knowledge acquired by you during the weeks and months after the examinations were over. In other words, whenever you graduated to a higher level of learning and knowledge you would have found the earlier stuff childish.

But always remember this for a fact that you are where you are today only because of those 'imperfect answers'.

Had you not given those answers within the permitted timeframes, you probably would have remained stuck with the same questions or answers in the same situations.

Life moves on. Time does not stop. What is important for an individual is to clinch the opportunity or the moment, within the limitations around him.

A decision taken at the right time, even if it is not cent per cent satisfactory, will yield a certain result. But a perfect decision taken a couple of days later may not yield any result at all.

Business situations in the corporate environment are all about taking decisions at the right time.

Therefore, it is important for us to always prepare a plan for the day and take decisions based on the information and resources available on that day and not wait for another two-three days expecting some more information and resources to become available. Not taking the decision for two-three days may have serious implications for the organization you work for. Therefore, it is to be understood that we, as managers, must learn to take decisions as per the given situation, based on the experience and knowledge available as on the day rather than try to stall a decision with some excuse or the other based on the possibility of acquiring some more information at a later date.

I strongly believe that there is no perfect plan.

It is said that the famous painter M.F. Hussain, whose rise in popularity and saleability is attributed to the series called 'white horse paintings', came across these paintings in somebody's house and asked the house owner to let him touch up the paintings for making some improvement. It goes to show that there is always scope for improvement. But then, there is also a particular 'period' within which the improvement works. If Hussain were to keep on touching up the painting in order to achieve some illusory idea of a perfect series of horse paintings, he might have been stuck there. He would have missed the 'opportunity bus'.

The Pareto principle or 80/20 rule explains the perfection trap numerically. For example, it commonly takes 20 per cent of the full time to complete 80 per cent of a task. It takes 80 per cent of the effort to complete the last 20 per cent of the task. Achieving absolute perfection may be impossible. Since enhancing the effort results in diminishing returns, further activity becomes increasingly inefficient.

Remember, a good plan is always better than the perfect plan. And, today is the day!

12

Dreams are nothing but a wish that you wanted to come true

Most of the young graduates who join business enterprises have a dream. This dream transforms into a wish. The wish then is systematically broken down into tangible goals.

It is very important for you to break your dream into small steps, convert these steps into your goals, set a timeframe for these goals in the framework of the overall career growth that you envisage to achieve, and then plan your strategies to achieve these goals.

It is important to understand and accept that you may often be 'criticised' as a dreamer. But, believe me, there is no individual who achieves success in life and who has not been a dreamer.

Dream you must! And you must dream big!

Being realistic means not to dream about something which does not look like ever being achievable.

Dreaming big, you grow bigger, personally and professionally.

Dreaming big is perfectly compatible with clarity of purpose and the ability to fix targets.

Execution is the essence of dream fulfillment.

You should be clear as to how you wish to achieve the various targets in order to realize your dream.

Therefore, you should clearly lay down all the action steps you need to take to fulfill your wish and to realize your dream.

Divide your wishes and goals into calibrated segments and go forward one step at a time until you realize the big dream you had envisioned.

'People seek immortality, whether they are aware of it or not.
People do want to "live" in the memories of others.'

'Every individual should make an effort to see his worth through the eyes of others, using them as his mirrors.'

'Great management gurus find humility to be perfectly compatible with fierce resolve and strong leadership.'

BOSS. I CANNOT HANDLE IT WITH MY LIMITED EXPERIENCE.
PROBLEM
EXPERIENCE

13

If a problem cannot be solved, enlarge it

I have always followed this dictum given by one of the most admired Presidents of the United States of America and one of the most successful Generals in history, Dwight D. Eisenhower. And I have hugely benefitted from it.

As Chief of the American and Allied forces during the decisive phase of the Second World War and as US President at the height of the Cold War, Eisenhower must have dealt with an unimaginably large number of complex problems. He emerged victorious in the Second World War and led the US through one of its most turbulent times. Under his leadership, the US emerged as a very robust economic and military power. In fact, one of his several initiatives, the Interstate Highway System, is one of the most high-impact developments in the history of the US.

When Eisenhower says that if a problem cannot be solved, you should enlarge it, we should take it as a sacred commandment.

Some problems can be easily solved or directions can be given to a team to find solutions for these problems. But most of the time you grapple with difficult situations in the naturally complex business environment.

Situations are dynamic, often intermeshed and sometimes running their independent course.

Based on your experience and learning from different sources, you develop a subconscious pattern of responding to situations. This response often takes care of the situation which would otherwise have developed into problems.

As a manager, it is your job to anticipate if a situation can become a problem and keep a close watch on it.

If your experience tells you that a situation has the potential of growing into a problem, you would use your learning to chalk out a roadmap, in advance, with your subordinates. You would give them an indication about all the dimensions of the problem and, accordingly, they would develop a problem-solving plan.

There would also be entirely novel situations. Drawing upon your past experience of handling numerous situations, knowing the capabilities of your subordinates, using your grit and determination, you will be able to solve such a first-of-its-kind problem as well.

If by any chance you are not able to solve the problem, never push it under the carpet and expect the problem to get solved on its own.

In a business environment, problems never get solved on their own. Rather, they often grow into larger problems, affecting the organization far more adversely.

One of my colleagues sent me this quote of Susan Del Gatto, which makes great sense, 'If you choose not to deal with an issue, then you give up your right of control over the issue.'

It is, therefore, important that you highlight the problem at an early enough stage.

Today, you have very effective tools which allow you to send across the problem to your seniors. If you feel that it will not be possible to communicate it effectively enough through such communication tools, meet the seniors and discuss the problem with them. Everyone will provide his own perspective on the situation and would try to come up with different ways of solving the problem.

When you analyze and put together all the suggestions, ideas and perspectives, you will most probably find a solution which is workable.

'You have to "personify" your job into a living and throbbing thing pulsating with possibilities, excitements, challenges and accomplishments.'

'Enjoy the perennial source of energy that your work, nay, your love, is!'

'Always let your team members know that you follow the spirit of the motto, "What E'er Thou Art, Act Well Thy Part."'

We must take hard decisions.
Tactics
STRATEGY

14

In the corporate world, you are selected, not elected

In Indian society, we are generally brought up with the approach of adjusting to the environment. We are imbued with the spirit of accommodation. We generally do not want to antagonize people around us, so much so that many a time we end up making compromises.

Look at the Indian joint family system—a great social and cultural institution with its unique features! Any new entrant into the family puts up with a lot and accommodates quite a bit, in his or her efforts to get accepted in the extended family. This kind of a joint family setup has people of different ages, different levels of education, different ways of thinking, angularities, prejudices, views on life and their opinion as to how the new family member should conduct herself.

When you enter a joint family which is fair and good and which wants you to adjust to its requirement, you accept the adjustment also.

In a way, the various members in the large joint family become the 'constituencies' of the new member and she takes care of their aspirations and expectations pretty much as a people's representative does in his political constituency. Tolerance, accommodation and appeasement are part of the strategy to achieve the objective of remaining popular and acceptable.

But, in the corporate world, you are not in the business of maximizing your acceptance and popularity; you are in the business of maximizing shareholders' returns. And, you have to understand that you have been selected to head a department or head an organization to serve the overall organizational objective. You have not been elected.

Your decisions should be based purely on the business interests of the organization, the industry and in view of the overall goal that your department or the organization wants you to achieve.

Here, it is not desirable to keep everybody happy or adjust to everybody's wishes and demands.

You must have clarity as to what you want and how it can be achieved, even if it means rubbing someone on the wrong side now and then. At the same time, when you set out on this journey, please remember that this approach also takes you to a situation where there is a very thin line between being assertive and being brash. Your sensitivity, your self-reflection, your keeping the feet firmly on the ground will enable you to choose the correct path.

Despite the shift towards flatter organizational structure and sharper focus on teamwork, what remains unchanged is that companies are very much like fighting units aiming for larger chunks of the business territory and commercial victories in the marketplace. Most of the terminology of business planning like strategy, tactics, etc. are borrowed from the world of defence. And, it is pure common sense that a fighting unit cannot be run on the basis of decisions and methods accepted by the majority. Just like the general takes his call, the business leader also needs to back himself and go ahead. Just as the general is not elected to be the chief of the army staff, so is the business leader not elected as the CEO of a company.

'The idea behind the strategy of not waiting for the best is to not take too long, else the battle is lost.'

'Life moves on. Time does not stop. What is important for an individual is to clinch the opportunity or the moment, within the limitations around him.'

'Dreaming big, you grow bigger, personally and professionally.'

MEETING
ROOM

15

Pete rakhle goon kore; koee phele khoon kore

Hold it within yourself, and earn credit; speak out, and get destroyed

This is something my grandfather, the late Sanjeeb Chandra Roy used to tell us very often. I forget the precise context in which he would say this. But as I grew up and faced the world I realized that it is actually a valuable management tip.

Often during management discussions and meetings that you have attended, you might have spoken out of turn only to feel belittled. You would have repented a thousand times as to why you did not hold your thoughts and ended up looking like a fool.

Did you face a situation when you felt very angry at someone, yet you did not let it all out, and let the moment pass? Later, you realized that the situation was not directed at you at all. Had you blurted it out you would have stepped out of line and might have antagonized your boss or a very important person who has had a very important role in your life.

As managers, when you are called to important meetings, be sure that you are well prepared, have thoroughly read the background papers and done in-depth research before making any interjection.

‘In a business environment, problems never get solved on their own. Rather, they often grow into larger problems, affecting the organization far more adversely.’

‘In the corporate world, you are not in the business of maximizing your acceptance and popularity; you are in the business of maximizing shareholders’ returns.’

‘Companies are very much like fighting units aiming for larger chunks of the business territory and commercial victories in the marketplace.’

SUCCESS
CUSTOMER SATISFACTION

16

If you don't care, your customer never will

Business leaders and management gurus generally subscribe to a customer-centric view of the business world. Some important statements by a management guru and some business leaders bear this out.

'The purpose of business is to create a customer.'

—Peter Drucker
(from *The Practice of Management*)

'There is only one boss. The customer. And he can fire everybody in the company from the chairman on down, simply by spending his money somewhere else.'

—Sam Walton
(from Michael Bergdahl, *The 10 Rules of Sam Walton: Success Secrets for Remarkable Results*)

'It is not the employer who pays the wages. Employers only handle the money. It is the customer who pays the wages.'

—Henry Ford
(from *My Life and Work*)

'Our DNA is as a consumer company—for that individual customer who's voting thumbs up or thumbs down.'

—Steve Jobs
(from Tyson McCann, *The Art of the App Store: The Business of Apple Development*)

Ultimately all these business thinkers conclude that no business entity can exist without satisfying its customers. This is similar to the saying which I frequently hear from Permanent Way Inspectors (PWIs) of the Railways. I have heard PWIs saying, 'I take care of the track and the track takes care of my job.' The work of PWIs in the Railways is to inspect the railway tracks and certify them as rail worthy. If accidents occur, they result into losses not only to the railways or the economy but to the country as a whole.

Sometimes, under the garb of professionalism, people believe that a task well performed is enough for the success of the organization. I cannot vouch for the international customers but I can say from my little experience in the Indian context that a good job is not done unless the customer is satisfied.

We, the managers, are familiar with the ISO terminology which says that meeting the customers' stated need and implied need is important. The fundamentals of quality management, with customers and other stakeholders at the centre, are published by the International Organization for Standardization. Commercially speaking, satisfaction of the customers forms the basis of any business.

It is the implied need that is more important for a manager to understand in satisfying his or her customer. This is where the attributes of caring, understanding, relationship building, communication, frequent interaction, receiving feedback and responding to feedback make one manager more successful than the other.

If the goal of the business enterprise is ultimately to sell its products and make money, then it is also the role of the manager to see that customers not only buy the products once or twice but become regular users of the organization's products and services.

Every manager who wants to promote his business, needs to understand the customer's requirements not only on the basis of the stated needs which are explicitly described in the work order or the technical specifications but also through an assessment of the implied needs of the customer. The implied needs could include quick response to defect rectification, quick reaction time from the maintenance team, basic courtesy and friendliness, public information about the various solutions and options, complaints not being passed around, dedicated attention and respect.

It is quite possible that in a contract for construction of a building, the technical specifications do not explicitly cover the safety arrangement for workers to be provided by the builder. But the implied need of the customer would be that there be no accident or death during construction. This can only be taken care of by having strong systems for safety, including work-ways, safety-nets, safety-belts, work-protocol and by ensuring that the workers are educated and trained to understand the safety systems and take necessary precautions.

The manager's job is to quickly identify the implied needs related to a particular assignment not only at the time of work on a product or starting an order but right at the beginning, i.e. at the time of preparing price bids of the quotation so that, in addition to the stated needs, the implied needs of the customers are also taken care of.

Some managers feel that all this has cost implications and may make their commercial pitch unacceptable to the customer. But if you look around, you will find that there are enough examples where the customer is interested in placing repeat-orders on the specific organizations not only because of the cost benefit aspects but for the comfort and reliability they derive from the assurance that these vendors would meet both the stated and implied needs.

Customer being the king, it is to be assured that not only his stated needs but also implied needs will be met.

17

If you don't blow your own trumpet, someone else will use it as a spittoon

When the American humorist Will Rogers (*Go for the Gold: Thoughts on Achieving Your Personal Best*) says, 'Get someone else to blow your horn and the sound will carry twice as far', he is far off the mark in the corporate context. Here, you have to honk your own horn and blow your own trumpet.

From the time you enter the competitive world, beginning with your entry into school, you vie for attention, approval and acceptance from your teachers.

In this eagerness of striving for acceptance and appreciation you not only continuously improve on what you do but you also try to impress your teachers by your good behaviour, your responses, your presentation and above all, by informing your teachers, from time to time, of what you have been working on, based on their directions and guidance.

When you enter the corporate world, you start working at a junior level as one among many people performing somewhat similar work and reporting to the same boss. The effort should be to do well and also get noticed, and be seen as a person who is a step above—a cut above the rest.

This can be done only if what you do, how you do it, and what you achieve must be projected at the right time to the right person.

Imagine a situation when you have completed a group task in which your contribution has been the key to achieving the breakthrough. Also, suppose you have not taken any further initiative to inform your supervisor as to how it was done. But instead of you, your colleague has given this information and cornered all the credit and appreciation. I am sure, if you look at your entire career span, you would find many such instances.

I do not intend to recommend the kind of credit hogging which proves detrimental to team spirit or performance orientation. Never.

The most effective and ultimately beneficial approach is to do productive hard work and make concrete contribution. But having done that hard work and having made that contribution, you should not remain a wall flower or a doormat. And, importantly, do not let anyone else mask your contribution. Therefore, it is good to do well and also speak up for yourself at times.

I also do not recommend the approach of being pompous or arrogant. You have to be a good performer. Humble. A team player. At the same time, you need to be capable of conveying your role and contribution with clarity, confidence and grace. If you do not do this, your not-so-generous colleagues may manage to keep you perpetually hidden in the background and utilize your hard work for their self-promotion in the eyes of the superiors. Never let that happen.

And it is for this reason that I recommend that occasionally you must blow your own trumpet. I am happy to know that management experts also subscribe to the common sense wisdom contained in the motto, 'If you don't blow your own trumpet, someone else will use it as a spittoon.'

LEARNING

18

Live as if you were to die tomorrow. Learn as if you were to live forever

Mahatma Gandhi, Father of our Nation, said, 'Live as if you were to die tomorrow. Learn as if you were to live forever'. The great leader and visionary who led India to independence said this many decades ago, even before people of my generation were born.

When we try to comprehend what he had said, we appreciate how relevant his saying is even today. It will remain relevant forever.

The Mahatma said that you should learn to live life as if you were to die tomorrow. Thus, he urged us to make the best use of the day that the Almighty has given us. It begins with the first rays of the rising sun and the chirping of the excited birds and ends only when you decide to call it a day.

In every second, every minute, there is an opportunity to learn from what you see, from what you feel, from what you hear and from what you are taught.

The second part of the Mahatma's advice is to 'learn as if you were to live forever'. It says you should absorb everything that you learn during the day, store it properly in the hard drive of your brain, mark it and archive it in such a fashion that you can retrieve it anytime you need it. Thus, you keep on adding to the repertoire of your skills and knowledge.

It is important to remember that learning never ends.

Every day, every moment, you learn either because you want to learn or because of the subconscious absorption of knowledge by your brain through other senses even when you are not conscious of it.

It is also important to know that we are living in a time in which everything is moving at a frenetic pace. Technology is changing very fast, knowledge is getting obsolete or upgraded, beliefs and convictions which held sway only a few years ago are no more relevant, and resources which were the basis of our work at one point in time have become irrelevant today.

The world has become flat and seamless, thanks to Information Technology (IT).

In July 2013, newspapers carried features about the end of the telegram in India. Rest in peace (RIP) telegram.

Continual change calls for continuous learning and adaptation. Absence of it causes iconic companies like Kodak to become almost extinct.

The bottomline is to never stop learning. This is the only way to renewal of professional knowledge. This is the only way to keep the business sustainable.

Nama
kirtan

19

Gurujee's teachings

Karo prane jano byatha nahi di
May I never hurt anyone's soul
Karo pran jeno hori na loi
May I never take anyone's life
Nikhilo praneeke apon janiya
May I consider all beings as my own
Bhalobashi dhele pran
May I love all, pouring my heart out
Ei chai Bhogoban
This is what I yearn for, O Lord!

These lines are taken from a *namakirtan* (hymn praising the Lord using His holy names) which my Guru Maharaj Jee Sree Sree

Mohananand Brahmachari sang for us. I imbibed it deeply in my childhood.

I never consider this as only a namakirtan. I look at it as an advisory for my life. As I grew older, I realised that these were words of management wisdom as well.

As a manager, whose survival is linked to targets and goals, you have to make the best use of the resources at your disposal. Productivity of material resources can be measured through a defined 'input-throughput-output' process. But human resources, which play a key role in your achieving targets, do not allow for such a mechanical, predictable and precisely measurable process.

Karo prane jano byatha nahi di

May I never hurt anyone's soul

Is it possible that you lead a collective of human beings and also follow this advisory of not hurting anyone's soul?

You must realise that *pran* or soul of an individual is a very sacred element within his core.

This 'pran' is very sensitive and sensible. It is not superficial. It can separate the genuine need from the perceived need of the individual. It is also the seat of conscience and, hence, can differentiate right from wrong.

As a manager, when you reprimand a person for not having performed to your expectation:

- Never hurt his soul
- Never speak in a derogatory manner beyond the context
- Never make personal remarks
- Never reprimand him in front of subordinates
- Never use unparliamentary language
- Always be ready to 'forgive and forget' after the reprimand

This approach goes a long way in developing a team and building trust. Your subordinates will understand the sensitivity and concern behind your reprimand. They will try to correct themselves, accepting the reprimand as a learning experience rather than resorting to sulking and de-motivating others.

Be a well meaning boss!

Karo pran jeno hori na loi

May I never take anyone's life

How is this a management lesson?

Please remember that every time you become instrumental in someone's dismissal or removal from a job, you have actually taken the 'Pran'—the life out of that very person's existence in the organization.

There is a very common Hindi idiom '*pet pe laat maarna*' which means snatching away one's livelihood. This amounts to an extreme form of violence in the corporate context.

It is your responsibility as a manager to see that every resource works towards the identified goal. If you have been allocated two vehicles, one brand new and the other a few years old, would you not use the brand new one to undertake long journeys and the older one for shorter routes? Similarly, every person can fit into your scheme of things and no one is to be discarded. Your ability as a good manager is to find the right slot for him and then motivate him. Help him break his goal into smaller targets and allow him to take baby steps, holding your hand.

Nikhilo praneeke apon janiya

May I consider all beings as my own

To be a successful team leader you have to become both 'father' and 'mother', for your team. Then the team would look up to you for guidance, support, and appreciation and would also accept reprimand when required or justified. If you stand on this psychological foundation, you are a complete leader and also a parent. Love will flow from you to each and every team member, just like parents' love which reaches out to all the children, without any expectation of return, without any distinction between achiever and non-achiever.

Bhalobashi dhele pran

May I love all, pouring my heart out

Remember that the people who work with you keep striving for your appreciation—a small gesture of love from you now, and a small word of praise then. Learn to demonstrate it through your body language and see how they respond.

Ei chai Bhogoban

That is what I yearn for, O Lord!

This may appear to be only a religious statement. But it is not so. 'Bhogoban' or the Lord here does refer to God. But the management essence is in 'Ei chai', i.e. in your intense wish. Who are you wishing for?

For yourself. Thus, at all times you are training your mind, your actions and your entire being into wishing for being capable of:

- Never hurting anyone's feelings
- Utilizing everyone's potential through effective hand-holding
- Operating from a 'nurturing parent' state, impartially and with affection
- Expressing appreciation through positive strokes

'What you do, how you do it, and what you achieve must be projected at the right time to the right person.'

'Before anything is accomplished in concrete terms, it is conceived in the mind, with clarity and purity, by the true achiever.'

'On achieving your "goal", treat it as a small step towards larger goals that you aspire for.'

Sankalpa Shuddha Hi Siddha.
INTEGRITY
HONESTY
STRATEGY

20

Sankalpa shuddha hi siddha

If your intentions are pure, you are bound to succeed

The key words, '*sankalpa*', '*shuddha*' and '*siddha*' are taken from Sanskrit, the language which is a great repository of ancient wisdom. Of wisdom validated in effective action through the millennia!

Spiritual masters continue to spread such wisdom by way of imparting their blessings upon disciples. These blessings are for the rounded growth of disciples through pursuit of the four ideals of *artha* (economic wealth), *dharma* (pursuit of principled growth), *kama* (appropriate satisfaction of desires) and *moksha* (salvation).

'Sankalpa' is known as 'goal setting' in the management jargon. In Sanskrit, it connotes the initial resolve at the beginning of an important activity with a specific goal.

All management gurus say that success cannot be achieved without setting a goal. When you make a 'sankalpa', be it at the initial stage of your life regarding your academic performance, during your professional pursuit at a later stage for your career growth, and later in a managerial position for the growth of the organization, you have to set goals. 'Sankalpa' encourages you to set goals.

'Shuddha' means 'pure'.

In management jargon, 'shuddha' could be 'pure intention' or 'clear objective'. When you set your goal, you know best how to filter the goal so that it becomes achievable. Thus, 'shuddha sankalpa' means that you have not only set a goal but you have also taken care to set such a goal which can be achieved.

'Siddha' means, 'completed, achieved, accomplished'.

In management jargon, it can be simply described as 'self-actualization'.

When you achieve 'siddhi' under a 'sankalpa', that is, when you achieve your goals, it becomes important to remember that you may have achieved a milestone, but it is a small step towards the larger steps that you need to take in life following the motto 'Sankalpa Shuddha Hi Siddha'.

This is what my esteemed Gurujee imbibed in me right since my childhood so that it got etched in my consciousness that one has to structure a goal, split and filter the goal into achievable targets and be humble about the achievements, considering them to be but the baby steps to the larger goal of self-actualization which, in spiritual terms, is called 'moksha'.

Like any pithy aphorism, 'Sankalpa Shuddha Hi Siddha' lends itself to different meaningful interpretations. A person, well versed in Sanskrit, may say that the expression would mean, 'a person with pure intentions is the one who achieves the exalted state of a liberated one.'

This interpretation of the expression is in harmony with the simple meaning which focuses on the power of intentions in achieving results. In fact, it is very much about the power of pure intentions.

'Sankalpa' also means strong mental resolve. Before anything is accomplished in concrete terms, it is conceived in the mind, with clarity and purity, by the true achiever.

Man's landing on the moon was first conceived as a clear possibility by space scientists. And later, it became a small step in the great space voyages which mankind has been undertaking since then.

In the context of an organization, the clarity and purity of vision takes place in the mind of the leader or the doer.

Clarity of vision and purity of mental resolve transform into results.

This simple and fundamental process or truth has been analyzed by management gurus in different ways and expressed in different terminologies at different points in time.

Thus the learning points contained in this aphorism are:

- Set a goal at every stage in your life
- Chart out a roadmap to achieve your goal by laying down 'achievable targets' and clear strategy
- On achieving your 'goal', treat it as a small step towards larger goals that you aspire for

About the author

Arup Roy Choudhury, a doctorate from Indian Institute of Technology Delhi, is presently the Chairman and Managing Director of NTPC Limited, which is the largest power generator in India and one of the ten largest power companies in the world.

During his illustrious career spanning more than 34 years, Dr Arup Roy Choudhury has been holding the position of Chief Executive Officer (CEO) for over 12 years. In April 2001, at the age of 44, he became the youngest CEO of a central public sector enterprise in India—the National Building Construction Corporation Limited (NBCC). He turned NBCC around from a loss-making company unable to pay salaries and earmarked for sale to a '*Miniratna*' profit-making company, paying dividends to the Government. During his tenure in NBCC, Dr Arup Roy Choudhury also undertook several landmark projects spread all over India, including the General Pool Residential Accommodation at New Moti Bagh Complex at Delhi, the CBI Headquarters building, the Civil Services Officers' Institute (CSOI), and the National Press Centre for Ministry of Information & Broadcasting at Delhi.

Dr Arup Roy Choudhury has earned many accolades and received several awards over the years. Some of the major awards conferred upon him include 'Best Organizational Turnaround' from the Hon'ble President of India in 2006, 'Best Individual Leader' of a Public Sector Enterprise from the Hon'ble Prime Minister of India in 2010, and the 'Gold Trophy' for NTPC for Best Performance from the Hon'ble Prime Minister of India in January 2012.